THE INTO

CONDUCTING JOB INTERVIEWS

A Sterling Paperback

SIT-Management Series
An Imprint of
STERLING PUBLISHERS PRIVATE LIMITED
L-10, Green Park Extension, New Delhi-110016
Ph.: 6851023, 669560, 660904 Fax: 6851028

Conducting Job Interviews by Jagjeet Singh & Adrian Holden
©1997 Federal Publications Sdn. Bhd. Malaysia
First Indian Reprint 1997
ISBN 81 7359 109 1

Published by Sterling Publishers Pvt. Ltd., New Delhi-110016.
Printed at Baba Barkhanath, New Delhi.

Introduction

*C*ONDUCTING JOB INTERVIEWS has been written to meet the needs of those who have to carry out job interviews. The interview that is to be conducted may involve school leavers, fresh college and university graduates with no work experience or experienced employees seeking higher positions.

CONDUCTING JOB INTERVIEWS not only explains the purpose and structure of an interview but also guides the reader on how to prepare for the interview, good questioning techniques to follow, and finally what to do after the interview.

This book is divided into six easy-to-follow chapters containing useful ideas and suggestions, and the much needed guidelines for successful approaches to conducting job interviews. Each chapter ends with a summary of the main points discussed along with an explanation of difficult and unfamiliar language.

A special feature of this book is the chapter devoted entirely to case studies. These involve a school-leaver, a fresh university graduate, and someone with work experience. Each case study shows what techniques are used to get the required information from interviewees and to hire the best person (s) for the job(s) advertised.

It is hoped that this comprehensive and easy to follow guide will help you get your ideal employee.

About The Authors

Jagjeet Singh

Jagjeet Singh boasts of 32 years of teaching English. During this time she has taught in schools, colleges, universities and conducted training sessions for corporations. Some of the courses that she has handled include The Interview Process, Job Applications, Writing Resumes, Effective Communications Skills and Memo Writing.

Adrian Holden

Adrian Holden has been teaching for the past 15 years at high school and tertiary levels in many different parts of the world. He has conducted courses such as Business English and Business Technical Writing. Currently he is teaching in a local institution.

Contents

CHAPTER 1

The Interview 1

The Job Interview 4

Purpose of the Job Interview 8

What Interviewers Look For 10

At a Glance 13

Terms You Need to Know 14

CHAPTER 2

The Pre-Interview Process 15

Working Out the Job Profile/Requirements 17

The Job Advertisement 19

Screening and Shortlisting 30

At a Glance 33

Terms You Need to Know 34

CHAPTER 3

Preparation 35

Administration and Organization 38

Files 59

Questions 61

At a Glance 66

Terms You Need to Know 67

Contents

CHAPTER 4

The Interview Process 69

Structure of the Interview 71

The Interviewer 84

Questioning Techniques 96

At a Glance 114

Terms You Need to Know.......................... 115

CHAPTER 5

The Post-Interview Process 117

At a Glance 131

Terms You Need to Know.......................... 131

CHAPTER 6

Case Studies 137

Case Study One 135

Case Study Two 154

Case Study Three 174

1

one chapter one chapter one chap

chapter one chapter one chapter one

one chapter one chapter one chap

chapter one chapter one chapter one

one chapter one chapter one chap

chapter one chapter one chapter one

one chapter one chapter one chap

chapter one chapter one chapter one

one chapter one chapter one chap

chapter one chapter one chapter one

THE
INTERVIEW

THE JOB INTERVIEW?

Before we start, let us look at three important questions:

      1. What is a job interview?

      2. Who is the interviewee?

      3. Who is the interviewer?

WHAT IS A JOB INTERVIEW?

A job interview is a structured conversation/dialogue with the specific purpose of finding the best available person to fill a vacant job.

It is a face-to-face meeting between two or more people – employer(s)/the interviewer and prospective employee/interviewee.

WHO IS THE INTERVIEWEE?

That is the one who has applied for the job. The applicant who is called for an interview is there to convince and persuade the interviewer(s) that he is the right person for the job. The interviewee has to "sell" himself and present himself favourably to the interviewer.

WHO IS THE INTERVIEWER?

That is you! The interviewer is the person whose job it is to talk to people who have applied for a particular post. From all the people you talk to, you must choose the best one for the job.

Be human – do not terrify the poor interviewees!
Just make sure you get the best person for the job!

PURPOSE OF THE JOB INTERVIEW

WHAT ARE INTERVIEWS FOR?

This is your opportunity to meet the applicants face-to-face. You can really use the interview to get to know each of the applicants as a person, and to ask them some questions which will help you make a decision about them.

Once you have written the job advertisement, read the resumes of all the applicants and shortlisted the best ones, the time for the interview has arrived.

Fine, I can understand that. But what exactly should I find out about them?

During the interview, try to get as much information as possible on:

● Education

● Personal Qualities

● Suitability for the Job

● Experience and Career Aspirations

● Practical Matters

● Interests and Leisure Activities

● Family Background

PURPOSE OF THE INTERVIEW

Interviewers and interviewees attend interviews for different purposes. The table below tells you what their purpose is.

INTERVIEWER	INTERVIEWEE
• to get to know the prospective employee.	• to get to know the prospective employer.
• to discover more than what is stated in the resume and application form(s).	• to get to know more about the nature of the job/working hours/salary.
• to determine if the applicant is suitable for the job – is he the RIGHT person for the job?	• to find out if you really want the job.
• to see how effective the applicant's communication skills are.	• to show the interviewer you are the RIGHT person for the job.

• to gauge the personality and attitude of the applicant.	
• to match the specific job requirements with each interviewee's qualifications, personal qualities and experience.	

WHAT INTERVIEWERS LOOK FOR

Interviewers wish to employ someone who:
- is committed
- will give his best to the company
- will quickly fit in with the company
- will promote the company
- will stay on and grow with the company
- has effective communication skills
- will be a tremendous benefit to the company
- has leadership qualities and initiative
- has a positive attitude

- is very willing to work hard
- is willing to take up challenges
- has a good academic background
- has relevant experience where needed
- has the initiative to do things for the company if the need arises
- has a good image
- can be relocated

> Ah! These are the qualities I should be looking for! I know I will have a hard time interviewing all these shortlisted applicants. But that is the only way I can find out more about the applicants. That is my job!

Interviewers do not wish to employ candidates who:

- have no initiative
- are negative in their approach
- look untidy

- cannot express themselves well
- show little or no interest in the company
- are neither lively nor enthusiastic
- do not possess a strong, dynamic personality
- have not taken any trouble to find out about the company
- are here only to earn the money
- do not have a very good academic record
- do not know where they are going and what they want
- come to work late
- leave the office on the dot
- are not willing to sacrifice their time
- are not willing to work overtime
- cannot make decisions
- have poor communication skills
- have poor language ability

No! Not this one. His spoken skills are poor!

Not this one! He is wasting my time. Has no idea about the company. How can I employ him?

AT A GLANCE

❏ A job interview is a structured, face-to-face meeting between the employer and the applicant for a vacant job to establish whether the applicant is suited for the post and is better than other persons who have applied.

❏ The job interview enables the interviewer to meet the applicant in person and to really find out about the applicant and to get to know him or her better, before reaching a decision.

❏ It helps the applicant to sell himself/herself and to find out more about the job, the company and the conditions of work.

❏ Employers look for people who will benefit the company not for people who are in it for what they can get out of it!

❏ Employers look for a number of positive qualities in job applicants and those who exhibit negative qualities will not be given jobs.

TERMS YOU NEED TO KNOW

Applicant the person who formally applies for a job by telephoning or writing to an employer.

Committed devoted, willing to work hard for the success of the company.

Employee a person paid to work for a firm or for another person.

Employer a person who has other people working for him or her or a company that people are working for.

Initiative drive, enterprise; can work without being told; can take the lead.

Interviewee person being interviewed.

Interviewer person who asks prospective employee questions in an interview to see if the latter is the right person for the job.

Job advertisement an advertisement which invites applications from suitably qualified people to fill a vacant job.

Prospective future, potential.

To recruit to get new members of staff, to encourage people to work for your company.

To relocate to move one's place of work from one town to another.

Resume a person's bio-data or c.v. (curriculum vitae); a summary which gives details about one's past employment, education, qualifications etc.

To shortlist to choose a small number of job applicants from the large number of original applicants for a job.

chapter two   chapter two   chapte

chapter two   chapter two   chapter two

chapter two   chapter two   chapte

chapter two   chapter two   chapter two

2

chapter two   chapter two   chapte

chapter two   chapter two   chapter two

THE PRE-INTERVIEW PROCESS

chapter two   chapter two   chapte

chapter two   chapter two   chapte

chapter two   chapter two   chapter two

chapter two   chapter two   chapte

chapter two   chapter two   chapter two

WORKING OUT THE JOB PROFILE/REQUIREMENTS

Before you actually interview job applicants for any particular job vacancy, there are a number of essential steps you must follow first:

1. Working out the Job Profile/Requirements
2. The Job Advertisement
3. Screening/Shortlisting

Let us look at the very first step.

JOB PROFILE/REQUIREMENTS

Take your time.
Be systematic.
Be patient.
Make sure you
get it right.

I know what I need
because I have spoken
to the person who does
the job at the moment.

Good. Interview people doing the job to find out about:

1. **The Job Process**:   How the job fits into the rest of the company.

2. **The Job Function**:   What has to be done in the performance of the job.

3. **The Skills Required**:   The professional and personal skills/qualities needed.

> You can then develop a job profile which will include the personal and academic requirements of the job.

Now that you have worked out the requirements of the job, you can start to think about writing the job advertisement.

THE JOB ADVERTISEMENT

O.K. I will try to write an advertisement. But how ...?

Why not take a look at a few? You need to have some models to help you. Once you examine some carefully, you will soon realise that they have more or less the same structure.

ARCHITECTURAL
FIRM requires
experienced

a) DRAUGHTSMEN

b) ILLUSTRATOR

Interested
applicants are
requested to write
with resume and
photo to:
The Manager,
P.O. Box No. 818,
(NST D029),
80730 Downson

SITUATION VACANT

ST. PETER'S
SCHOOL
TULONG BRUNEI.

Seeks applications from
GRADUATED
–TRAINED TEACHERS
to teach:-

1. ENGLISH in
Secondary School.

Apply before
5th November 1993 with
telephone number to:-

THE PRINCIPAL,
ST. PETER'S SCHOOL
P.O. BOX 22, TULONG 5000
BRUNEI DARUSALAM.

ADMINISTRATIVE
ASSISTANT
wanted

Professional firm has
several vacancies for
senior and junior position.
Minimum qualification
– SPM with distinction
in English.

Salary: RM800–RM1,200
Call: 3395432

The structure of an advertisement is as follows:

1. Information about the company

2. Designation

3. The job requirements

4. Conditions of employment

5. How to proceed

Once you have studied a few advertisements you will realize that there is a set pattern. The points that you have to bear in mind when you write are to always be precise, exact and clear. Take your time and do not rush when writing an advertisement. Do not be afraid to use the samples to assist you. Look at the samples again and again if you need to.

Let me examine a few advertisements. Well, these have the same structure!

A long established garment manufacturing company in Singapore has vacancies for:-

Accounts Clerk

- LCCI Certificate
- Able to read and converse in Mandarin
- Able use computer/software e.g. Lotus
- With or without experience
- Min. 6 'O' level passes including English

Please write in confidence, giving full particulars of qualifications, working experience, current earning, expected salary and contact number to or call:

The Administration Manager
Bing Sun & Co (Pte) Ltd
80 Billings Lane, Singapore 2573
Tel: 3633222

Let me try to draft ... Name of the firm is simple. Now I have got to think of the job position. Well, I need an Assistant Manager (maintenance).

That is good. You are doing well.

The job names are specific. I must be clear about this.

LQM Technology Singapore

LQM, a fast growing high tech semiconductor production equipment and materials manufacturer with turnover in excess of US$100 million requires the following personnel:

① Information about the company

LEADFRAME SALES ENGINEER

② Name of the job

- University degree or advanced diploma in Engineering
- 2-3 years' working experience ideally in semiconductor manufacturing
- With drive and perseverance, a team worker
- Frequent short trips in the region required
- To be based in Singapore

③ Job requirement

Attractive salary, remuneration benefit packages and good opportunity for further career advancement will be offered to the right candidates.

④ Conditions of Employment

Please send full resume and recent photo, expected salary and contact number to:

⑤ How to proceed

**The Administration Manager,
LQM TECHNOLOGY SINGAPORE PTE LTD,
18 Holland Avenue 9, Singapore 2776.**

O.K. Now what were the other three parts of the advertisement?

THE LANGUAGE IN AN ADVERTISEMENT

RECEPTIONIST

We seek a bright, cheerful and experienced Receptionist with a good personality. She is expected to attend to phone calls and undertake some typing. She will also be required to undertake clerical work.

FACTORY ENGINEER

FINANCE & ADMINISTRATION MANAGER

OUR REQUIREMENTS

- Possess a professional Accountancy qualification such as ACCA or CIMA with some experience in a manufacturing environment
- Must be a team player with strong interpersonal skills and discipline
- Knowledge of PC application software such as Lotus 123 is essential

OUR OFFER

- A very attractive remuneration package will be offered to the right candidate
- An opportunity to participate in the growth of the Company.
- A five-day work week
- Other in-house benefits

Never do a job advertisement in a hurry. It will not save time in the long run.

Have it checked!

Where do I answer that question? Perhaps, I should put that here?

Who are the interviewees you are aiming at: English/Malay/Chinese/Indians ...?

That is much better.

Human Resources Executive

● At least possess a Certificate in Personnel Management or equivalent discipline
● At least 2 years' relevant experience in all aspects of the personnel/human resources function, preferably in a manufacturing concern
● Mature, possess strong leadership qualities and an analytical mind
● Possess excellent communication and interpersonal skills in Bahasa Malaysia and English, both written and oral

Having written the job advertisement, you have to think about placing it in the local papers. Yes, you need publicity. But for how long should you run the advertisement? Which newspaper do you advertise in?

In answer to the first question, take note that if you run the advertisement for three days in certain papers, they will give you free space for the following day. Do not miss out on such opportunities. One day is insufficient because the good candidates might miss the advertisement. As to the second question, this depends on the job. You must know what type of people read each newspaper. This will help you target your audience.

SCREENING AND SHORTLISTING

Now I have got all the applications. I am glad so many applied.

That is good. But how many of them are really qualified for the job? How many are suitable?

When the applications start to pour in, you need to work out what to do with them. Use the screening process to pick out those who are suitable for the position that you wish to fill. Firstly, separate those who have the qualifications from those who do not. This will be helpful as a smaller number of applications will be far easier to handle.

This is where things start to get difficult. You see, all are qualified. But who is most qualified?

What do I judge by? Appearance? Preparation? Some are better prepared. Others look better. Let us look at the forms. Some are neater and better presented. Appearance does tell you a lot about the type of person. Shall I throw away the untidy ones?

Well, I know some people who do that, but let us be more systematic than that. Let us start by looking at their personal qualities.

Personal qualities will help you narrow down your choice even further. Consider if the applicant is diligent or if he can work under stress. Think about deadlines. Do not forget to take his activities, interests and positions of responsibility he held previously into consideration.

Is that all? Can I now discard some according to academic and professional qualifications, and personal qualities?

There is still one more important criterion that you ought to consider. Can you make a guess at it?

The final factor you should consider is working experience. Decide if it is necessary for the person whom you wish to employ. Once you have weighed all these factors against the applications you would have narrowed down your choice considerably. The next step would be to grade the remaining candidates.

You grade the candidates by shortlisting (arriving at a shorter list of people) them. Arriving at a shorter list of people to interview will make your job easier. But you must see the persons on the list before making a final decision. When you meet them you will be able to decide on matters such as whether they are able to communicate or not. The more candidates you interview, the better even though you will find it to be tedious, time consuming and not to mention expensive. However this is the only way you will be able to get the best person for the job.

AT A GLANCE

❏ Time needs to be taken to work out exactly what type of person is needed to fill a job vacancy. This can be best achieved by producing a job profile.

❏ Many job advertisements follow a similar 5-point structure. This includes information about the company, name of the job, the job requirements, the conditions of employment, and how to proceed with the application.

❏ If an employer follows these five steps, is careful with his choice of language and has his final draft checked, then the job advertisement produced should interest a good number of suitable applicants.

❏ The advertisement should be placed in a newspaper which is read by the type of person likely to be interested in applying and for a sufficient number of days for enough suitable applicants to be aware of the vacancy.

❏ When all the applications have arrived, it is likely that there will be more applicants than you have time to interview. The applications, therefore, need to be screened and shortlisted to make the task of the interviewer manageable.

TERMS YOU NEED TO KNOW

Application form the paper on which there are particular questions (usually details about the applicant) and spaces marked for an applicant to write the answers to them.

Conditions of employment conditions of service; job requirements such as hours, duties, etc. and benefits such as salary, holidays, etc.

Draft a copy of something written. A writer usually produces several drafts before he makes the final copy.

Job profile a thorough description of a job including process, function and requirements.

Job requirements job specifications.

Personal qualities characteristics/personality of an individual.

Screening examination of applications to ensure they fulfil requirements.

Shortlisting selecting the best candidates from a large number of applications.

3

PREPARATION

Now that you have successfully completed the pre-interview process, that is, you have worked out the job profile/job requirements, the job advertisement, and have screened and shortlisted the suitable applicants, you have to prepare for the interview proper. There are three broad areas you should look into before calling the applicants for the interview, namely:

      1. Administration and Organization

      2. Files

      3. Questions

ADMINISTRATION AND ORGANIZATION

This is an essential part of any interview, and the more thorough the preparation, the more smoothly the interview process will be on the day of the interview and during the actual interview. The following will have to be looked into with some care:

- Time-tabling of interviews
- Informing the shortlisted applicants
- Briefing and informing the clerical staff
- Preparation of the interview room
- Preparation of the waiting room
- Reception of candidates
- Choosing the interviewer(s)

TIME-TABLING OF INTERVIEWS

Once you have shortlisted the candidates you may start thinking of interviews. Some interviewers are extremely impatient
and try to schedule all the interviews for the very next day!
Though it is good to get things done quickly, this is not
advisable. Conducting proper interviews take time. Moreover
you have to bear in mind that you may be free the next day
but more importantly the candidates may not. It would be far
better to work out a tentative time-table of the interviews.

No! No! A time-table is a must! You have got to be more organized. You need to know how long it will all take ...

A tentative time-table? But why? I will call them all here tomorrow, and whoever is here can come into the room first, and whoever is not here, we will forget about them — on a 'first come, first served' basis.

A time-table of the interviews is a must if you wish to be more organized. You should estimate how long each interview will take and inform the candidates of the time accordingly. Avoid asking all of them to come in at the same time. You may think that this will make selecting a suitable employee easier but this is not true.

Think of what would happen if all the candidates came to your office for an interview at the same time. The only way you would be able to see all of them would be to call the whole lot of candidates in together, take a look at them and decide who is the most suitable person. When you imagine this scene, does it not remind you of a beauty pageant rather than an interview? Try to have a proper system and organization for selection. It will take up your time but it will be worth the effort.

9.30 – 10.15 am	ROBERT
10.30 – 11.15 am	JAMES
11.30 – 12.15 pm	KELLY
L U N C H	
2.30 – 3.15 pm	ROSE

A time-table of interviews! Yes, that seems the right thing to do; but why did I not think of that? I was going to send out letters or even get my secretary to call all of them in on the same day without realizing how difficult and impractical it would have been! You need some experience in these things before you can organize things better.

A time-table is not difficult to make; but before you start making one, ask yourself some questions.

Can you think of these questions?

Ask yourself these questions to help you draw up your interview schedules:

- How many minutes do you need for each applicant?

- Do the interviewers need a break in between and for how long?

- How much time do you need to assess each candidate after the interview?

Time to assess after each interview? For what?

You cannot be a genius and remember all at the end of the interview. You have to make notes on each one as you go along after every interview.

Take note of the number of shortlisted candidates there are and for how many days you wish to conduct the interviews. When alloting time for each candidate do not forget that some candidates may be from far off places, so you should be fair and give them sufficient time to bring out the best in them.

Generally, 30 minutes should be ample time for each candidate. However if there are many candidates you may have to cut the interview time to 20 minutes. On the other hand, if the number of candidates is small you may wish to spend more time on each person. The important point to remember here is that the interviewers may not be able to concentrate for long without a break. Put aside adequate time for breaks.

INFORMING THE INTERVIEWEES

The next step is to call the applicants in for the interview by telling them that they have been shortlisted and are invited to attend an interview. Refrain from setting up the interviews at your convenience only. Check to see if the applicant will be able to make it.

Some interviewers argue that if the applicant is really interested he will turn up no matter how incovenient it is. Otherwise the applicant is struck off the list. A shorter list will make the interviewers' task far easier but then and again you might just be striking out the best applicants in the list.

So, go step by step. The suitable applicant might have to travel some distance, look into his other schedules at his present place of work, take a day off; or at least a few hours to attend the interview. Therefore the applicants must be told in advance.

How much in advance do you think I should tell them? I have got no idea really!

At least one to two weeks depending on where they are staying or working.

That sounds reasonable. But how do I inform them? Which is the surest and quickest way?

The next thing that needs to be done is to consider how to inform them. Going through the application forms, you will find that each one has indicated a contact number. Some may have given their fax numbers. Others have given phone numbers and addresses. At times, some applicants wish to keep the interview confidential, so they prefer to be contacted by letter.

Contact them in one of the following ways:

● By fax

● By phone

● By letter

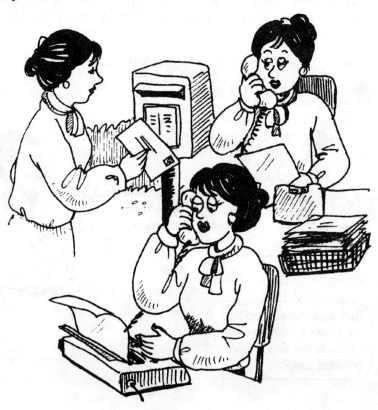

Not all the applicants may be able to make it on the specified day and time. There may be important things that they need to do or perhaps there are no bus tickets, etc. Therefore, it is important for you to state in the form that should the interview date and time be unsuitable, they should get in touch to arrange for another convenient day or time. Make some allowances on the time-table.

Once the replies come in you can finalize the schedules and make copies for the receptionist and also for the various notice boards to indicate to the interviewees their actual times of the interviews and which rooms the interviews will be held.

What about the venue – the interview room and the waiting room? Have you decided on that?

I. must look into that first. Conference Room 1 will be the best.

Factors to consider when choosing an interview room:

- It is the right size.
- It is air-conditioned.
- The chairs are comfortable.

Is there anything else you want to tell them?

Yes, I have got something on my mind. Do I tell them to bring any documents or testimonials?

Original documents are a must. You need to verify the results and other relevant information given to you in the form.

BRIEFING AND INFORMING THE CLERICAL STAFF

I have sent out all the letters to the shortlisted applicants. That is a big job done and now I can just wait for the day of the interview to meet all the applicants face to face.

I am afraid that meanwhile, you have got a lot to do.

You will have a lot of things to do before the actual day of the interview. For instance, you have to brief the clerical staff. You must brief them adequately beforehand; do not leave things until the last minute. Get your staff to prepare the files for the interviews. Relevant information for each candidate is in each file for the interviewer to look at. Naturally, these files will hold the application forms and testimonials. The interviewer will make notes during the interview and leave them in the respective files.

Assign duties to your clerical staff. Decide who will put up signs/arrows to the interview room. Who is bringing in drinks for the interviewers? Who will be in charge of the waiting room? These are some of the many little things that should be seen to early.

PREPARATION OF INTERVIEW ROOM

There are four important considerations when preparing the interview room, namely:

● Selection of the room

● The furniture

● Positioning of the furniture

● Signs to indicate an interview is in session

Let us deal with these step by step.

❶ Selection Of The Room

The room that you select should be:

● **Quiet**
Always avoid a noisy environment.

● **Unoccupied**
Ensure that no one else is going to use it or you will find
yourself moving from one room to another!

● **Comfortable**
Ensure that the air-conditioning and lights are working.

● **Clean and tidy**
Check to see that curtains are clean, waste-paper baskets
and ash-trays are emptied. Do note that no one should
smoke during the interview – not even the interview panel.

❷ The Furniture

It all depends on the environment you are trying to create. Sometimes the distance between the interviewer and the interviewee makes it too formal. That is why today more and more interviews are conducted without the use of a table or desk. In the case of the latter there is no distance between the interviewer and the interviewee, and the atmosphere is quite informal and friendly. This helps as the candidate is naturally more relaxed. The table or desk is like a barrier. So, it all depends on you.

❸ Positioning Of The Furniture

The candidate and interviewer could be sitting facing each other at some distance. Or, even side by side but facing each other at an angle. If you do not use a desk, then you will need some hard board to write on, for you certainly need to make some notes during the interview.

> How do I arrange the desks? Where does the candidate sit? Where do the interviewers sit? In a row or in a circle?

If there is a panel of interviewers you will probably need some tables or desks. In this case, it is best they have some desks and sit behind these facing the candidate.

4 Signs To Indicate An Interview Is In Session

No candidate likes to be interviewed in a noisy setting. It can be very nerve-wracking and certainly far from conducive and comfortable. Also, there should be no interruptions when an interview is in progress.

There is nothing more disturbing and depressing than being interrupted just when you are trying very hard to impress and make a point clear. To prevent interruptions put up signs that say **"SILENCE"**, **"INTERVIEW IN PROGRESS"** or **"PLEASE DO NOT DISTURB!"** The signs will let others know that there is an interview in progress so that they can be a little more considerate. Candidates are generally very nervous so we should be as quiet as possible.

❺ Preparing Waiting Room

Having prepared the interview room, you should now turn your attention to the waiting room. Early comers need a place to wait before they are interviewed. Some may have travelled on an overnight coach and would probably be exhausted. They would definitely need a comfortable room to wait in.

The room does not necessarily have to be air-conditioned but if it is then all the better. It would be ideal if it were next or adjacent to the interview room. Above all, it must be neat and comfortable with some reading material for candidates to browse through while waiting their turn.

⑥ Reception Of Candidates

Choose a receptionist to welcome the candidates when they arrive for the interview. Do not simply pick anyone who happens to be free. The person must be someone who attended your briefing for the clerical staff; someone who knows what is happening.

The person should have a friendly nature, be pleasant and alert at all times. It goes without saying that he/she should also be efficient as quick decisions might have to be made. For instance, there might be a message that someone is delayed. This means that quick adjustments have to be made to the time-table and the Panel Chief in the interview room has to be notified.

"Yes, I can shift Kelly over to this slot since she is already here, and ..."

CHOOSING THE INTERVIEWER(S)

And now we are ready to begin the interview.

But who are your interviewers? Have you given a thought to that important person or persons who is going to make a difference to your company?

Decide on whether the interview is going to be conducted by a single person or by an Interview Panel. This is very important for various reasons.

If you should decide on only one interviewer, ask yourself who the most suitable one to do a good job of recruiting is. This person must have the experience and skill in deciding who the best person for the job is. A very good experienced interviewer is better than many inexperienced ones.

However big firms with many special divisions might need an Interview Panel. There would be a specialized person who heads a particular section to gauge how much the interviewee knows. This will depend on the vacancy.

Whether the interview is conducted by one person or a panel, you would need good interviewers. Who makes a good interviewer? The answer is very simple. This would be the person who has interviewing skills and aptitude and who will take special care to organize and plan his interview. A structured interview is the best.

FILES

Are you sure we have prepared everything for the interviews? Let me see. Ah! the files; are they ready?

Files? What files? I do not remember any files!

Once the waiting room and the interview room are fixed, the clerical staff who have been briefed should "do their home-work" in advance before the actual day of the interviews. Among other things, the files of all the interviewees have to be prepared. This can be a laborious job as it is very time-consuming. Every file should have certain essential documents.

CONTENTS

The file should contain the following:

- application form or c.v.
- any correspondence relating to the job interview
- certified copies of certificates
- certified copies of testimonials
- references
- other related information

ARRANGEMENT

Name and number each file according to the order of appearance for the interviews. Check this against the interview schedule to ensure that the order is correct.

As for the arrangement of documents in each file, place the application form or c.v. at the top. This is to be followed by certified copies, testimonials and list of referees. Be systematic, that is do the same for all the files. Every file should have the same order of arrangement inside.

How many files must you make for each candidate? This depends on the number of interviewers. If it is a one-to-one interview, then you just need one file. However if it is a panel, it is not necessary for all the interviewers to have all the documents in their files. All that is needed is one complete file with all the documents in it for the Chairperson of the panel. The others only need a list of names each, and the c.v. or the application form.

The person in-charge of the files and the documents will have a time-consuming job to do. This is why you cannot leave this aspect of the interview for the very last minute. Making copies of the c.v.s or application forms may take hours.

QUESTIONS

Now that the individual files of interviewees are ready for the interviewers for the day of the interviews, there is only one other area that has to be attended to, and that is the most essential part of any interview – the QUESTIONS that will be asked at the interview to pick the best person for the vacant post.

I have so many questions in my mind. I do not think I will have any problems. Why do I need to prepare in advance? It is such a simple job!

No, that is not the best way to conduct an interview.

You will find it worth your time to structure the interview questions. In the short time that you have with the candidate, you will have to decide if the person is the best one for the job. It will be impossible for you to make the best use of the interview if you do not prepare or structure your questions.

ORGANIZE QUESTIONS

Think about the kind of questions you want to put forward. It is always best to use open-ended questions at interviews. These questions may also be called Wh-questions. The questions ask for a lot of information and the candidate is forced to speak. This way you can find out more about his knowledge.

Wh-questions help you know more about the candidate's:

● language abilities

● skills of communication

● analytical abilities

By using wh-questions you will be able to find out more about the candidate's achievements, his failures and also why he is leaving the job. This is most important as this is your only opportunity to meet the candidate face-to-face.

Study the examples of Wh-questions given.

WH-QUESTIONS

● What sort of experience do you have in this field?

● What would you do if you are caught in such a situation?

● Why did you choose to major in this field?

● Why do you think the experts felt that ...?

- When was the last time that you handled ...?
- When is a good time to start ...?
- How would you have handled such a situation?
- How did the economic situation affect your company?
- Where do you think would be an ideal place to set up a factory producing such products?
- Which of the products do you like best?
- Which one of these options would you choose?

Make it a point to avoid yes-no questions. Questions of this sort will not get you much information out of the candidates. The candidate will merely give you a yes or no answer. If you still need more information, you will be forced to put forward another question to the candidate. This is not only tiring but it will also take up a lot of time. Remember, you do not have much time with the candidate.

QUESTIONS TO AVOID

- Have you ever had such an experience?
- Should the person have handled it in that manner?
- Do you agree with the experts?
- While at Kim, Jim and Tim, did you face such problems?
- That is not the way to do it, is it?
- Did you major in this field?
- So, you are interested in banking?

CHECKLIST

Do a checklist. This will ensure that every area is questioned before the candidate leaves the room. Checklists actually make it easier for the interviewer(s) to have things planned out in detail. And do not forget that the better the planning, the better the interview.

The questions that you plan should cover the following areas:

- edcuational background
- academic background
- professional background
- family background
- personal qualities
- suitability for job
- career expectations and aspirations
- candidate's expectations
- candidate's interests
- candidate's leisure pursuits

CHECKLIST

- Educational background
- Academic background
- Professional background
- Family background
- Personal background
- Suitability for Job
- Career expectations and aspirations
- Candidate's expectations
- Candidate's Interest
- Candidate's leisure pursuits

Right. I feel I have covered all aspects. I am now ready to conduct the interviews.

But do not forget, if there is a Panel, decide who should ask which question. Remember, it is very important to allocate question areas.

AT A GLANCE

❏ Pre-Interview preparation is an essential part of any successful interview process.

❏ Candidates should be asked about their availability for interviews well in advance, and a schedule of interview times written according to interviewees' availability.

❏ Interviewees should be informed by telephone, fax or letter of the date, time and place of their interviews.

❏ Clerical staff should be thoroughly briefed regarding their duties well in advance of the interview sessions.

❏ The interview and waiting rooms should be selected, prepared and suitably furnished in advance of the interviews.

❏ Timetables for interviews and "Please Do Not Disturb" signs should be placed in strategic positions.

❏ Special care should be taken to ensure that interviewees are greeted by a suitable, well-briefed receptionist.

❏ Interviewers should be carefully selected for the task of selecting the best person to fill the job vacancy.

❏ Files should be prepared containing all relevant documentation.

❏ Interviewers should carefully prepare questions to ask during the interview to cover the areas of education, personal qualities, suitability, aspirations, interests and family background.

❏ If a panel is interviewing, each member of the panel should be given an area or areas to focus on during the interview.

TERMS YOU NEED TO KNOW

Checklist a list of questions or areas of interest which the interviewer is to cover during the interview.

Interview environment the atmosphere in and around the interview room. It should be quiet, peaceful and inter-ruption free.

Interview period a group of interviewers who will together interview candidates for a job.

Venue the place where the interview is to be held.

Wh-question open-ended questions beginning with *when, who, what, why, where, which, when* and *how* which force the person being questioned to pro-duce lengthy answers.

ur   chapter four   chapter four   chap

chapter four   chapter four   chapter four

ur   chapter four   chapter four   chapt.

four   chapter four   chapter four

4

ur   chapter four   chapter four   chapt

THE

chapter four   chapter four   chapter four

INTERVIEW

PROCESS

ur   chapter four   chapter four   chap

chapter four   chapter four   chapter four

ur   chapter four   chapter four   chap

chapter four   chapter four   chapter four

When all of your pre-interview preparations are completed, you are now ready to interview the short-listed job candidates. This chapter will describe the structure of the interview itself, help you to think about the image you wish to project as an interviewer, discuss some of the **do's** and **don'ts** of interviewing and finally focus on the type of questions you should be asking your interviewees to make the best out of the time available.

STRUCTURE OF THE INTERVIEW

Most job interviews follow the same basic three-part structure:

● The beginning

● The middle

● The ending

Look at the tables on the next page which highlights the 3 stages of the interview and focus on the aims and contents of each stage with specific reference to the role of the interviewer.

THE STRUCTURE OF THE INTERVIEW PROCESS

Stage 1

The Beginning

AIMS	CONTENT	ROLE OF INTERVIEWER
• To welcome the candidate. • To put the interviewee at ease so that he can give his best. • To "get to know" the interviewee on a casual/informal level.	• Casual/informal opening conversation to 'break the ice' and allow the candidate to get over his initial nerves about the interview.	• Controller of interview • Welcomer • Ice-breaker

Stage 2

The Middle

AIMS	CONTENT	ROLE OF INTERVIEWER
• To clarify information given in c.v./application. • To clarify information about the job, responsibilities, conditions etc.	• The "heart" of the interview in which the interviewer(s) can set about the questioning task and discover if this interviewee is the person the company is looking for.	• Controller of interview • Questioner • Assessor • Provider of information

• To build up a true picture of the candidate. • To discover to what extent the candidate matches the job requirements. • To assess whether the candidate could fit in with/cooperate with the staff of the company.	• Information about the job itself must be clearly explained.	

Stage 3

The Ending

AIMS	CONTENT	ROLE OF INTERVIEWER
• To provide any further information the candidate may ask for. • To inform the candidate about further procedures. • To wind up the interview.	• Allow the interviewee to ask any questions he might have regarding the job and provide full answers. • Winding up of the interview, informing the candidate what will happen next. • Thanking the candidate.	• Controller of interview • Provider of information • Leave-taker

STAGE ONE: THE BEGINNING

As an interviewer, you have three main aims at this crucial stage of the interview:

● To welcome the candidate to the interview;

● To put the interviewee at ease;

● To get to know the candidate informally and build up a rapport between interviewer and interviewee.

Right. So it is my job to make him feel at home so that he can really show what he is made of!

You see, if you do not create the right atmosphere, the interviewee will not give a true reflection of his abilities.

One way to break the ice with a nervous candidate is to ask a number of informal or simple questions. The candidate will not feel threatened by these questions and begin to talk freely. The following questions are often used as ice-breakers.

Questions used as Ice-breakers

● How was the journey here?

● How did you travel down from Ipoh?

● How did you get to know about the job vacancy?

● Did you have any trouble finding our office?

Anything the candidate says is the chance for "small talk". Take the opportunity and show that you are a human being and build a rapport with the interviewee.

You have **3 important roles** as interviewer at this stage of the interview.

3 Roles of the Interviewer

● You must welcome the interviewee to the interview and, of course, to the company.

● You must 'break the ice' and try to make the interviewee feel at ease and allow him to show his true self.

● You must control the proceedings. You, as interviewer, must at all times be the person who sets the pace and direction of the interview.

STAGE TWO: THE MIDDLE

As an interviewer, you have **five main aims** at this stage, which is the longest stage of the interview.

Five Main Aims

● To clarify any incomplete, unclear information found in the c.v. or application form or to seek further information on any points raised.

● To provide the interviewee with a clear picture of the job, its responsibilities, duties and conditions of employment.

● To begin to build a true picture of the candidate as a potential member of your staff.

● To discover to what extent the candidate's qualities and qualifications match your job specifications/requirements.

● To assess whether or not this person could fit in with the people he would be working with.

Do you see why this is usually the longest stage of the interview? There is so much to think about. Make sure your checklist covers all of the areas.

Yes, I see what you mean. It is certainly a lot for one person to handle. I must be really methodical. Now I can see the advantage of having a panel of interviewers!

Be prepared to seek clarification on matters arising in the c.v , application form or cover letter, such as:

- educational qualifications
- professional qualifications
- work experience
- nature of present job
- reasons for wishing to change job

And, of course, you must be prepared to provide the candidate with details about the job.

Details of the job that the candidate should know about:

- job specifications
- working conditions
- duties and responsibilities
- salary range and fringe benefits
- working hours and holidays

To help you assess the suitability of the candidate, you will probably ask questions covering the following seven main areas:

- education
- personal qualities
- suitability for the job
- experience and career aspirations
- practical matters
- interests
- family background

So, as you can see, you as the interviewer have a number of jobs to do in the Middle Stage of the interview.

Indeed, you have **4 important roles** as interviewer at this stage of the interview:

To Control

● You must again control the proceedings of the interview. Especially in this long stage of the interview it is you who must lead and structure the questioning to ensure you can get the most out of the interview.

To Question

● You must question your interviewee thoroughly and methodically so that you have enough information on which to base your judgements.

To Provide Information

● You must provide information regarding the job.

To Assess

● You must assess the information you have collected and begin to make judgements regarding the suitability of the candidate for the job.

STAGE THREE: THE ENDING

As an interviewer, you have **3 main aims** at this final stage of the interview:

● To provide any further details the candidate may ask for regarding the job applied for.

● To inform the candidate about what will happen next in the job application process.

● To round off the interview by thanking the interviewee and saying goodbye.

You see, there is still quite a lot involved in this last stage, particularly if the candidate is very keen on the job.

Yes, and it means I really need to have all the details about the job at my finger tips.

Be prepared to answer any questions regarding the details of the job, such as:

● duties and responsibilities

● salary and fringe benefits

● working hours and holidays

● working conditions

● prospects of promotion

● the company's future plans

But if you are unable to answer a question, admit that you cannot and promise to find out the answer and send it to the interviewee.

You have **3 main roles**, then, in this final stage of the interview:

To Control

● You must continue to control the proceedings to the very end of the interview.

To Answer

● You must answer all questions asked by the interviewee to the best of your ability.

To Wind Up

● You must wind up the interview by thanking the interviewee and, if necessary, even seeing him out of the interview room.

Now I know all about the three stages of the interview. But, how do I know when to move from one stage to another?

A very good question. I always follow some simple guidelines.

STAGE 1 Move on when you feel the interviewee is at ease.

STAGE 2 Move on when you have gathered all the information you need to make an assessment of the candidate.

STAGE 3 Wind up the interview when the interviewee has finished asking questions and you have nothing more to say.

THE INTERVIEWER

VARYING ROLES OF THE INTERVIEWER

As we just saw, the interviewer must be a very flexible person since during an interview he has a number of different roles to fulfil. They are:

- controller of the interview
- welcomer
- ice-breaker
- provider of information
- questioner
- assessor
- leave-taker

And what makes it even more difficult is that the interviewer is playing more than one of the above roles at any one given time during the interview!

SOME COMMON MISCONCEPTIONS ABOUT INTERVIEWERS

You need to remember the following misconceptions, exaggerated though they may be, that some interviewees have about the interviewer.

MISCONCEPTION	TRUTH
• The interviewer is a monster, a dictator or a sadist.	• He is a normal human being doing his job.
• The interviewer wants to trick the interviewee.	• He is actually there to help the interviewee do his best.
• The interviewer wants to scare and intimidate the interviewee.	• He wants to discover whether the interviewee can do the job or not.
• The interviewer wants to make the interviewee look stupid.	• He wants to help the interviewee prove that he is suitable for the job.
• The interviewer is there because he likes to see people suffer.	• He is there because his boss has told him to be there.
• The interviewer only knows what it is like to be in control.	• Nonsense! He has been on the receiving end of an interview too.

You might find some of the ideas ridiculous but let us face it, we all feel rather worried about what the interviewer is going to be like, especially if we are new to interviewing.

BASIC GUIDELINES FOR THE INTERVIEWER

Below are some guidelines the interviewer should bear in mind at the interview.

DRESS AND APPEARANCE

- You must look fresh and smell fresh.
- Your clothes should be neat and tidy.
- Your clothes should project the image of your company.
- You should be well-groomed.

BEHAVIOUR

● Remember that you represent your company in the eyes of the interviewee.

● Be polite and friendly.

● Be firm and stay in control.

● Be helpful,understanding and patient.

LANGUAGE AND VOICE

● Speak clearly and naturally.

● Make sure you are clearly understood.

● Sound business-like yet friendly.

SOME COMMON PITFALLS IN INTERVIEWING

DON'TS

○ Don't be biased. Sex, religion, politics etc. should be irrelevant in interviewing.

○ Don't be domineering.

○ Don't waste time arguing with the interviewee.

○ Don't be hasty in making decisions/judgements about an interviewee.

○ Don't interrupt an interviewee when he is trying to make a point.

○ Don't be impatient.

○ Don't be rude.

○ Don't talk too much.

○ Never lose your temper with an interviewee however annoying you may find him.

○ Never lose control of the interview. Controlling the interview is one of your main roles.

If you are guilty of any of the above, you should try to avoid them in future. They are really bad habits and lead to bad interviewing.

BODY LANGUAGE

Just as you will be looking for clues in the body language of the interviewee, you must be aware of your own body language. The interviewee has eyes too, remember that!

DOS

1. Lean slightly forward and maintain eye contact.

This shows interest and attention. Maintaining eye contact shows good manners.

2. Smile

This shows that you are friendly and easy going.

3. Put your hands in a natural and comfortable position.

This shows you are at ease, comfortable and confident.

DON'TS

1. Do not fold your arms or cross your legs.

This shows you are defensive and insecure.

2. Do not lean back

This shows you are not bothered and disinterested.

3. Do not look away.

This shows you are nervous and are trying to hide something.

4. Do not tap your feet or your fingers.

This shows you are nervous and impatient.

5. Do not grip your chair or clench your fingers.

This shows you are nervous and tense.

6. Do not cover your mouth.

This shows you have something to hide.

7. Do not keep changing positions or fidgeting.

This shows that you are nervous and insecure.

QUALITIES OF A GOOD INTERVIEWER

Though very few interviewers can claim to have all the qualities listed below, the following are desirable characteristics of the good interviewer.

QUALITIES

- Politeness.
- Patience.
- Ability to get on with people.
- Good communication skills.
- Good listening skills.
- Ability to control the interview.
- Good organization.
- Willingness to prepare thoroughly.
- Good judgement skills.
- Fairness.
- Be at ease with the interviewing task.
- Confidence in one's own interviewing skills.
- Knowledge about the job being applied for.
- Ability to ask meaningful questions.
- Warmth of character.
- Ability to balance a person's good and bad points.
- Ability to match job requirements to personal qualities.
- Consistency – your treatment of the first and fifteenth interviewee should be the same!

QUESTIONING TECHNIQUES

One of the major differences between a good interviewer and a poor interviewer is the type of questions he asks and the amount of information they generate.

I think I need to find out more about how to ask good questions!

Sure. Let us start by looking at the type of questions which are really not very useful.

TYPES OF QUESTIONS TO AVOID IN INTERVIEWS

CLOSE-ENDED QUESTIONS

Interviewer : *Do you enjoy your present job at Robinson's?*

Interviewee : *Yes, yes, I do. I enjoy it very much.*

Close-ended questions are usually not very fruitful since they usually produce *Yes/No* responses and little more.

However, whilst not being very useful in themselves they do have a role to play in the job interview if used sparingly and carefully.

- They are simple to answer and are useful at the ice-breaking stage of the interview when the interviewer is searching for openings for small talk.

- They can be sometimes used as a lead into further questions of a more probing nature. (See probing techniques).

LEADING QUESTIONS

Interviewer : *Now, John, I am sure you do not have problems communicating with junior staff, do you?*

Interviewee : *No. no, of course not.*

Leading questions force the interviewee to take a position dictated by the interviewer. Either in the way the question is formulated or by the tone of the interviewer's voice, the interviewee is given little option but to follow the leading question.

- The leading question can reveal very little about the interviewee.

- The leading question actually reveals far more about the interviewer than about the interviewee.

LOADED QUESTIONS

Interviewer : *How do you feel about these **ridiculous** new personnel training techniques?*

Interviewee : *Well, hmm ... I am not too keen on them actually.*

A loaded question has a word or phrase in it or is said in such a tone that indicates the interviewer's attitude and dictates the interviewee's expected response. Again the poor interviewee is given little option but to follow the lead of the interviewer and condemn the new personnel training techniques as "ridiculous".

- The loaded question reveals very little about the interviewee.
- It reveals a lot about the beliefs and biases of the interviewer.

VAGUELY-PHRASED QUESTIONS

Interviewer : *Tell me what you know about personnel work.*

Interviewee : *Well, hmm... I do not know where to start really...*

And neither would most other people!

The question is too broad and fails to give the interviewee a framework in which to produce a clear response.

- Vague questions produce inevitably vague responses.

- Vague questions are often ill-planned and indicate that the interviewer has not organized his questions thoroughly enough.

So, I think you can see why these types of questions are not very useful in the interview situation. They just do not allow the interviewee to speak his mind.

Right. So what sort of questions should I ask to permit the interviewee to say what he thinks?

Well, there are a number of useful techniques in the next section which really force the interviewee to say what he feels. Let us examine them, shall we?

QUESTIONING TECHNIQUES USED BY SUCCESSFUL INTERVIEWERS

OPEN-ENDED QUESTIONS

Interviewer : What is it about your present job at Robinson's that you enjoy most?

Interviewee : Well, I think it is meeting people. You see, I love meeting people and at Robinson I not only deal with the company staff but I also get the chance to meet customers at their place of work...

The open-ended question gives the interviewee room to develop his ideas and really tell you what he thinks about a certain thing. In this way, you as interviewer get lots of information about the interviewee, his character, attitudes and suitability for the job.

Open-ended questions are usually preceded by the following "Wh" question words. Try to ask a few.

Wh-question words:
- where
- who
- why
- when

- what
- which
- how

Who has influenced you most in your life?

Which aspect of personnel work do you find most challenging and why?

Why do you wish to apply for a job at Wine & Whine?

How would you change the organization of your present office if you could?

When did you realise that you wanted to follow a career in marketing?

Where do you see yourself in this company in 5 years' time?

What are the main qualities of a good manager?

HYPOTHETICAL QUESTIONS

Interviewer :   *What would you do if your sales figures fell by 20% after you took over the post of Sales Manager?*

Interviewee :   *Well, I would have to analyse the reasons for this sudden drop in sales. There might be one single reason for the fall like a sudden lack of product appeal because our competitors have come out with a better model or there might be a number of factors contributing to the 20% fall such as...*

"What if" questions like this are a valuable technique when used at the right time in the interview.

- They make the interviewee "think on his feet".
- They show the depth of knowledge, experience and training the interviewee has to draw from.
- The hypothetical question should be used sparingly however.

The best "WHAT IF" questions are based on possible professional situations, are realistic and are answerable. Try a few!

What would you do if you had serious problems working with your new colleagues?

What would you do if the manager gave you too much workload?

How would you react if your boss took away some of your responsibilities and gave them to a junior?

PROBING TECHNIQUES

There are times during an interview when the interviewer will wish to probe more deeply into an aspect of the interviewee's suitability for the job. At times like these the interviewer may use one or a combination of the four techniques listed below:

1 Repetition of Key Idea

Interviewee : *..., and so I decided to concentrate on bookkeeping...*

Interviewer : *Bookkeeping?*

Interviewee : *Yes. I decided that bookkeeping would be a suitable area for me to specialize in since...*

You see how the interviewer is able to probe more deeply simply by repeating the key word "Bookkeeping"?

2 Silent pause

Interviewee : *... and so I decided to concentrate on bookkeeping*

Interviewer : *....*

Interviewee : *You see... I felt that bookkeeping would be a suitable area for me to specialize in since...*

Again, you can see how the interviewer forces the interviewee into a further explanation simply by maintaining silence for a short time.

3 Request for examples

Interviewee : ... and so I felt I had a lot to offer the company in terms of initiative and drive.

Interviewer : Can you give me some examples of how you put your initiative and drive to good use?

Interviewee : Yes... well, one example of this is when I decided to upgrade our promotion campaign by calling in a well-known firm of Public Relations specialists...

You see how the request for an example forces the interviewee to back up his claim with concrete proof... which he does very well.

4 Wh-probes

Interviewee : ... *and so I felt I had a lot to offer the company in terms of initiative and drive.*

Interviewer : **How** *did you help your company with your initiative and drive?*

Interviewee : *Well, thanks to improved promotion campaigning, the company ...*

Interviewer : **Why** *did you focus on the promotional side of things...?*

Interviewee : *Because it was one of the areas I had identified as a weakness in our company...*

Interviewer : **When** *did you begin to benefit from improved campaigning?*

Interviewer : *After about three months of solid campaigning, we...*

Interviewee : **Which** *product was the first to benefit?*

By using a series of Wh-questions the interviewer can really probe in depth into an area of special interest.

INTERVIEWER'S FAVOURITE QUESTIONS

When you begin the process of serious questioning in the Middle Stage of the interview, you will most probably form your questions on the seven areas of interest mentioned earlier in this chapter. The areas cover the following categories:

● education and training

● personal qualities

- suitability for job
- experience and career aspirations
- practical matters
- interests and leisure activities
- family background

Look at the open-ended questions often asked by interviewers in the seven areas and judge how useful they might be for you.

QUESTIONS ABOUT EDUCATION AND TRAINING

- What changes would you make in your school/college/university?

- What did you learn from life at school/college/university?

- What subjects did you like best at school/college/university? Why?

- In what way(s) did school/college/university prepare you for work?

- What did you like most/least about school/college/university?

- Why did(n't) you go to college/university?

- To what extent are your grades a true reflection of your ability?

- If you had the chance what changes would you make to this country's education system?

QUESTIONS ABOUT YOUR PERSONAL QUALITIES

- What are your greatest strengths and weaknesses?

- How do/did you get on with your school-mates/college-mates/work-mates?

- What really brings out the best in you?

- How would you describe yourself?

- What has given you most satisfaction in life so far?

- What is your definition of success?

- How do you perform under pressure?

- Tell me about the biggest problem you have had to face in life. How did you overcome it?

- We all make mistakes in life. What have you learned from yours?

QUESTIONS ABOUT SUITABILITY FOR JOB

- What is your ideal working environment?

- What appeals to you about this job?

- Why do you think you would be good at this job?

- Why did you apply to this company?

- What do you think the ideal relationship is between a boss and his staff?

- Tell me what you like about this company.

- What have you learned from your present job (past part-time job)?

- What things are most important to you in choosing a job?

- How do you think you could make a contribution to this company?

- How would you change the company you are working for now?

- Explain to me why I should give you this job.

QUESTIONS ABOUT CAREER EXPERIENCE AND ASPIRATIONS

- What is your ideal job at this stage in your life?
- What do you expect to be doing in 5–10 years' time?
- Why do you choose a career in.......?
- If you do not get this job, what do you plan to do?
- Why do you want to leave your present job?
- What do you like best/least about your present job?
- What have you gained from your present job that would help you in this one?

QUESTIONS ABOUT PRACTICAL MATTERS

- How do you feel about working long hours (overtime)?
- How do you feel about keeping deadlines and working under pressure?
- How long have you been driving?
- How do you feel about being relocated?
- What starting salary would you expect?
- When would you be able to start work?

QUESTIONS ABOUT INTERESTS AND LEISURE ACTIVITIES

● How do you spend your time when you are not studying/ working?

● What is your main leisure interest?

● Which of your hobbies/activities are you particularly good at?

● Have you ever organized activities for other people?

● What do you read most?

● Who is your favourite author? Why?

● What benefits do you think you get from your activities?

QUESTIONS ABOUT FAMILY BACKGROUND

● What does your father do for a living?

● What do/does your parents (wife) think about your applying for this job?

● What do your brothers and sisters do?

● How does being married affect your mobility?

AT A GLANCE

❏ Most job interviews follow a basic three-part structure consisting of beginning, middle and ending sections.

❏ The beginning section of the interview is the place at which the interviewer puts the interviewee at ease and tries to create a rapport with him/her.

❏ The middle section of the interview is the phase during which the majority of the important information is gathered on which the interviewer bases his judgement about the suitability of the interviewee.

❏ The ending section of the interview is the phase in which the interviewee is able to ask questions about the job he is applying for and the interviewer winds up the interview.

❏ The duration of each of these steps will depend very much on the interviewer's assessment of how the interview is progressing.

❏ The roles of the interviewer are many and vary during the course of the interview.

❏ Though interviewees are often apprehensive about attending job interviews, the interviewer is there to facilitate the smooth running of the interview and give each candidate a fair chance of proving his worth.

❏ The dress, appearance, behaviour and language of the interviewer all reflect the image of the company and the importance of the job interview.

❏ The interviewer must be careful to avoid a number of common pitfalls of interviewing and must be in control of his body language.

- There are a number of questioning techniques which allow the interviewer to discover a great deal about the interviewee's attitudes, character and suitability for the job.

- Interviewers tend to focus their questions on seven main areas of interest:
  - i) Education and Training,
  - ii) Personal Qualities,
  - iii) Job Suitability,
  - iv) Experience and Career Aspirations,
  - v) Practical Matters,
  - vi) Interests and Leisure Activities,
  - vii) Family Background.

TERMS YOU NEED TO KNOW

Assessor someone who judges specific qualities in another, a judge.

Biased prejudiced, unfair.

To break the ice to begin to be friendly with a person you are meeting for the first time.

Domineering bossy, controlling others excessively.

Fringe benefits perks one enjoys when holding a certain position or responsibility.

Hasty done in a hurry, too quick

in making a decision or choice.

Hypothetical not true or real.

Ice-breaker a person who tries to be friendly with another to put them at ease.

To probe ask questions to get certain specific information.

Rapport feeling of agreement and understanding.

Small talk conversation about small, unimportant things.

To wind up to finish, to end.

5

THE POST- INTERVIEW PROCESS

The period after the interviewing is over is a time for:

● Considering the relative merits of each candidate.

● Evaluating each candidate as a possible future employee.

● Making a decision as to whom you should employ.

● Communicating with all candidates to let them know whether or not their applications have been successful.

Let us look at each of the above post-interview tasks to see how to go about them.

MERITS OF CANDIDATES

> After each interview is over, you should allow yourself time to consider the strengths and weaknesses of each candidate.

One very easy and efficient way of recording your impressions is by using a simple checklist. The checklist should cover all areas you consider important with respect to the job being applied for.

Checklist

- Education
- Personal Qualities
- Suitability for the Job
- Experience and Career Aspirations
- Practical Matters
- Interests
- Family Background

Under the above general headings you may wish to include a number of more detailed sub-headings.

Two simple methods of using the checklist can be seen below.

Method 1

Personal Appearance

Very Poor	Average	Excellent

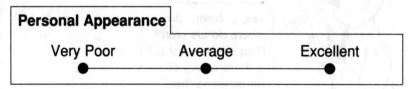

Method 2

Personal Appearance

Poor	Fair	Average	Good	Very Good	Excellent
			X		

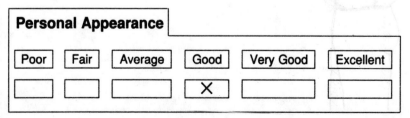

EVALUATING CANDIDATES

Now comes the more difficult part. You need to evaluate each candidate in terms of his/her potential for successfully doing the job advertised.

Yes, ... hmm... So, where do we start? How do we do that? Is there a way of determining that?

We start by going back to our job specifications and seeing to what extent each candidate matches up to the requirements.

We need to remember that job specifications and requirements come under three categories:

● **essential** – candidates *must* have these requirements

● **preferred** – candidates *should* have these requirements

● **advantageous** – candidates *may* have these requirements; it is good if they do have them but not necessary

So a candidate who has all the essential requirements is in a strong position.

That is right. One who has the preferred and advantageous requirements but lacks essential requirements will probably not stand much of a chance.

QUALITIES	REQUIREMENTS
• 4 years experience. BA (Hons.). Dip. Accountancy.	• ***must*** – have 3 years experience. – have BA (Hons.). – have Prof. Qualification.
• English, Cantonese, Hokkien. Has own P.C. Open, friendly person.	• ***should*** – speak English & Cantonese. – be computer literate. – be a good communicator.
• No knowledge of area. Able to drive.	• ***may*** – knowledge of area advantage. – asked to drive.

When the qualities a candidate has match the requirements of the job, we have a very strong candidate for the post!

Yes. What we need to do now is select the candidates who satisfy our requirements and either appoint them all, call them for a second interview, or decide on the best.

You may have enough vacancies for all the good candidates in which case your task is simple. If you have a limited number of jobs you may want to invite the best candidates back for a second interview. You may be satisfied that the information you have about the applicants is sufficient for decision making.

DECIDING

You now have to compare the candidates with one another to discover who is the best suited for the post.
The decision making process will again be based on matching what each candidate has to offer with what the specific job requires of its holder.

Interview Board

If you are part of the Interview Board you will probably be involved in post-interview discussions.

● You may be asked to award marks for candidates.

● You may simply be asked to name the interviewee you think is best for the job.

● The chairman may want to make the final decision.

One Interviewer

If you are the only interviewer then the decision is yours alone.

● It would be effective for you to devise a grading system based on your checklist.

● Whatever you do, be fair to all candidates by being as objective as you can.

And do not forget — a decision to give someone a job takes you very little time, but the results of the decision will be obvious to everyone in the company for years to come!

INFORMING CANDIDATES

Now, for the final step in the interview process. Informing all the interviewees of your decision.

Yes, but we are only really interested in the successful applicants, are we not?

This is not true. Even though someone has not been given the job, they have a right to a polite letter informing them so.

These days more and more employers send letters of rejection which actually explain to the applicants why they did not get the post.

Look at the job **Offer Letter** and the **Rejection Letter** to see what the typical letters look like.

JOB OFFER LETTER

J I T J A T

Mr. Brown
No. 18, Rd. 17/92,
Petaling Jaya.   20 August 1994

} Interviewee's address

Dear Mr Brown,

        Further to your interview of August 13th, I am very pleased to offer you the post of Accounts Clerk with our company. Congratulations!

} Offer

        As mentioned in the interview, you should start work on September 15th, and your starting salary will be $700 with overtime allowance and bonuses payable where applicable.

} Details of offer

        Please contact me as soon as you can to confirm your acceptance of our offer by September 1st. I look forward to hearing from you and feel confident that you will be a success in our company.

} Request for confirmation

Yours sincerely,

Brian

G. H. Brian
Accountant

REJECTION LETTER

JITJAT

Mr. B. White,
No. 23B, 5/72,
Petaling Jaya.   20 August 1994

Dear Mr White,
          We have now completed our selection interviews for the post of Accounts Clerk. Unfortunately, I have to inform you that your application has not been successful this time.
          The Interview Board feels that your experience was not sufficient for a post of this type. We would be pleased to receive further applications from you in the future.
          We thank you for your interest and hope that your job search will prove successful.

Yours sincerely,

Brian

G. H. Brian
Accountant

} Interviewee's address

} Sympathetic rejection

} Reason

} Expression of best wishes in future job search

AT A GLANCE

❏ Time should be spent systematically recording impressions of each interviewee.

❏ One efficient and easy way of doing this is by using a checklist.

❏ Candidates should be evaluated with reference to the requirements of the job they are applying for.

❏ The best candidates may be called for a second interview, all could be offered jobs (if available), or need to be compared so that a final decision may be reached.

❏ Rejection letters should be written in a positive and sympathetic way.

❏ Offer letters should be functional but express a feeling of pleasure at the prospect of mutual benefits.

TERMS YOU NEED TO KNOW

To evaluate to assess the abilities of a candidate.

Merits strong points, strengths.

Offer letter letter of appointment; letter in which a job is offered.

Post-interview after the interview.

Rejection letter letter in which a person is informed that he/she has not got the job applied for.

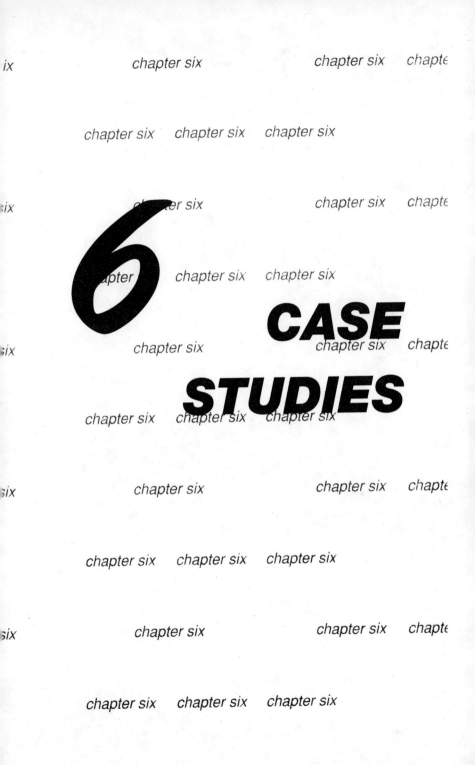

6 CASE STUDIES

CASE
STUDIES

CASE STUDY ONE

Mr Raj Ganesan – Administration and Accounts Manager of Easyware Household Distributors.

Susan Sim – 17 year-old school leaver applying for the Data Entry Clerk.

ABOUT THE JOB

The first interview is a school leaver applying for her first full-time job. She has just completed Form Five and has got 6 'O' Levels.

COMPANY	: DIY HOUSEHOLD DISTRIBUTORS
NAME OF JOB	: DATA ENTRY CLERK
APPLICATIONS	: 50 applications received; 10 shortlisted
VACANCIES	: 3
NATURE OF JOB	: Data Entry Clerk
EXPANSION PROGRAMME	: Sales department expanding – looking for school leavers to join in this expansion programme. No experience required. On-the-job training will be provided by the management.
PERSONS TO CONTACT	: Mrs Jody/Mr Tim

REQUIREMENTS : 'O' level or equivalent; typing and knowledge of computing an asset; good command of English; no experience required but willing to work hard; has a pleasant personality; can do overtime – is mobile.

DATE OF JOB : Immediately but negotiable.
COMMENCEMENT

Let us see how Mr Ganesan, the interviewer, handles the interview with young Susan. She will probably be a little nervous to begin with.

THE ADVERTISEMENT

D I Y
Household Distributors

DATA ENTRY CLERK
3 VACANCIES

DIY – a wholly owned subsidiary of the Giants of Today Group is responsible for the distribution of household ware throughout Asia. Due to rapid expansion we invite suitable applications for the position of DATA ENTRY CLERKS.

Requirements

● Minimum SPM or equivalent
● Proficiency in typing is an advantage
● Preferably having certificate in Computing
● Experience is not essential
● Good command of English

Call Mrs Jody/Mr Tim at 883920 or write in with detailed resume, stating current salary level and contact number enclosing 2 recent passport-sized photographs to:

The Administrative & Accounts Manager,

D I Y Household Distributors,
Lot 666, Jalan 33/45,
Subang Hi-Tech Park,
43600 Shah Alam.

not later than 25 November.

THE APPLICATION LETTER

1685 Rose Avenue,
Straits Gardens,
53400 Melaka.

8th July 19_ _

Mr R. Ganesan,
The Administration & Accounts Manager,
DIY Household Distributors,
Lot 666, Jln. 33/45,
Subang Hi-Tech Park,
43600 Shah Alam.

Dear Mr Ganesan,

I was very interested to see your company's advertisement for the job of Data Entry Clerk which appeared in The Star on July 7th, since I believe that I have the right academic background and practical experience for the post.

I am well aware of DIY's reputation as one of the most progressive companies in the household field and I have seen the quality of your goods for myself. I would like the opportunity to work for such a company. I have recently successfully completed my SPM examination and have also got a certificate in typing. For a number of years I have had my own computer and computing is one of my main interests in life. Whilst waiting for my SPM results, I worked as a temporary data entry clerk. My qualifications, experience with computers and a good knowledge of English seem to match the job description in your advertisement.

I have enclosed my completed application form and am available for an interview at any time. Please contact me at 06-934256.

Yours sincerely,

Susan
(Susan Sim)

APPLICATION FORM

DIY
HOUSEHOLD DISTRIBUTORS

APPLICATION FOR THE POST OF: *DATA ENTRY CLERK*

SECTION ONE: PERSONAL INFORMATION

Full Name [Capital Letters]: *Susan Sim*

Date of Birth: *10 August 1976*   Age: *17 years*

Place of Birth: *Melaka*   Nationality: *Malaysian*

Sex: *Female*   Religion: *Muslim* .

Identity Card Number: *763380*   Marital Status: *Single*

Full Postal Address: *1685 Rose Avenue*
Straits Gardens
53400 Melaka

Telephone Number: Office: _____–_____
Residence: *06-934256*

Languages [Tick (✓) the appropriate box]	WRITTEN Fluent Good Fair	SPOKEN Fluent Good Fair
1 Malay	✓ ☐ ☐	✓ ☐ ☐
2 English	☐ ✓ ☐	✓ ☐ ☐
3 _____	☐ ☐ ☐	☐ ☐ ☐

SECTION TWO: INTERESTS

Interested in computers: spend a lot of my spare time using my personal computer at home and have become conversant with word processing, data bases and spreadsheets. Keen netball player: represented my school.

(1)

SECTION THREE: EDUCATION

(Begin with most recent educational qualification first)

Name of Institution	Dates Attended		Qualifications Obtained	Date Awarded
	From	To		
Convent Secondary School, Melaka			SPM: English – C3 Malay – C3 Maths – C3 Geography – C4 History – C6 Religious Studies – C5	
Convent Primary School				

SECTION FOUR: PROFESSIONAL QUALIFICATIONS

Name of Institution	Dates Attended		Qualification Obtained	Date Awarded
	From	To		

(2)

SECTION FIVE: WORK EXPERIENCE

Name of Employer	Job Title & Description	Dates of Service		Monthly Salary
		From	To	
	Temporary			*RM400*

SECTION SIX: FURTHER DETAILS

(Use this space for any further details which will support your application)

It is my intention to study part-time towards a formal computing qualification. Although I have a good background in the use of computers, I feel it would be useful for me to gain some theoretical knowledge to add to my practical mastery. I would, therefore, hope that my future employer would support me in my efforts to improve myself professionally.

SECTION SEVEN: REFERENCES

FIRST REFEREE:
Name: *Mrs. J Fernandez*
Address: *3, Jalan Muar*
Kampong Gajah
54300 Melaka

Telephone: *06-499936*
Years Known: *7 years*
Position: *Headmistress*

SECOND REFEREE:
Name: *Mr Razali Osman*
Address: *4, Block A,*
Police Barracks
Jalan Johor
63700 Melaka
Telephone: *06-498700*
Years Known: *10 years*
Position: *Police Sergeant*

SECTION EIGHT: DECLARATION

I hereby declare that, to the best of my knowledge, the above information is true and correct.

Susan   *8/7*
_____   _____
Signature of Applicant   Date

(3)

ACADEMIC QUALIFICATIONS

- just 6 'O' levels.

WORK EXPERIENCE

- very limited but relevant: temporary job in uncle's firm.

PROFESSIONAL QUALIFICATIONS

- certificate in typing

ACHIEVEMENTS

- school prefect
- school netball team

PERSONAL DETAILS

- keen to do a computing course
- strong interest and background in computers
- good English

INTERESTS

- computers
- netball

These are the main points I have managed to find in Susan's occupation. I should try to find out more about them if time permits.

THE INTERVIEW

Let us study the following interview extracts and see how things develop.

THE BEGINNING STAGE

Interviewer : Good morning. Please sit down.

Welcoming the interviewee.

Susan : Good morning, sir. Thank you.

Interviewer : Could you tell me something about yourself?

A general "harmless" question to break the ice and allow Susan to start talking.

Susan : I am Susan from Melaka. I studied at the Convent and completed my SPM in December last year.

Interviewer : Oh, the Convent School! All of my sister's children went there. It is a very good school... they

See how Mr Ganesan takes the chance to indulge in small talk to put Susan at ease and show her that he is a "real" person with a family of his own.

always produce very good results, do they not? How was the journey?

Susan : Not too bad, thanks. I took an Express Bus. It does not take long now on the highway...

Another "easy" question to encourage the interviewee to talk informally about herself.

Interviewer : That is right. I often go down to Melaka to see my sister and her family. They live in Tanjong Kling... I see you live in Straits Gardens. That is not far away, is it?

Again the interviewer finds something in common to get Susan talking.

Susan : No, it is just a short walk away. I often go to the seaside for a walk when I am free.

Susan is talking quite freely now.

Interviewer : Right then, Susan, there are a few questions I would like to ask you about your application.

A clear signal that the time has come to move on to the more serious business of the 'Middle Stage'.

O.K. Try to see how Mr Ganesan applies some of the questioning techniques we have looked at.

THE MIDDLE STAGE

Interviewer : I see from the application forms that you have 6 'O' levels. Which are your favourite subjects?

Open-ended wh-question!

Susan : Well, I like Maths, Malay...

Interviewer : What about English? I see you have a C3 in English!

Probing with another wh-question to discover some important information.

Susan : Oh, yes. I like reading books. I think I am quite good at English especially Oral English.

Interviewer : I understand that you attended a typing course recently. Where did you take it?

Another wh-question to elicit information about Susan's typing course.

Susan : At an institute near my house. It was a

3-month course. I found it very practical.

Interviewer : Hmm... (nods his head).

Susan : I mean, I am really quite a proficient typist now and I have a certificate to show for my hard work too.

Interviewer : That will be of help. I see that you do not have any computing qualification.

Susan : Yes, it is true. I do not have any certificate in computing, but my dad owns a P.C. and I worked in my uncle's firm for some time. I have some experience of working with computers. I

Mr Ganesan has already read Susan's application form carefully. Here he gives her both the chance to talk about her practical computer experience and her desire to do a part-time computer course.

am actually going to take up a computer course during the weekends this month.

Interviewer : That is good. We need someone who has a working knowledge of the word processor at least. Your job here as a data entry clerk will require computing knowledge. Can you handle that? What have you done in that area?

Change of role from questioner to informer. Mr Ganesan begins to tell Susan about the job. Returning to Susan's practical knowledge of computers again.

Susan : Well, that is what I did in my uncle's firm, using spreadsheets and the like.

Interviewer	:	How do you think you benefited most from working at your uncle's firm?

Wh-question to find out what she did at her uncle's firm.

Susan	:	Well, ...

Interviewer	:	Do you know that this job is a 9 to 5 job and that at times you will be required to do overtime – of course, you will be paid accordingly for this?

Mr Ganesan again focuses on giving information about the job. Note how he is in total control of what is being discussed.

Susan	:	Do I have to work on Saturdays?

Interviewer	:	No, it is a 5-day week job.

Susan	:	I do not have to work on Saturdays, and that means I can take the computer course.

Interviewer : Yes, it would be quite convenient, would it not, Susan? Well, I do not think I have any more questions for you. Perhaps you would like to ask me something more about the job, Susan.

A clear signal that Mr Ganesan has now gathered enough information on which to base his evaluation of Susan and is now ready to move into the final stage of the interview.

Susan seems to be doing quite well. Let us see if she is still interested enough to ask more questions.

THE ENDING STAGE

Susan : Is there anyone else of my age working in the office?

It is the interviewee's turn to ask questions but Mr Ganesan, is still in control.

Interviewer : Yes, there are a number of teenagers in that particular office, so you would not be surrounded by old people like myself all the time.

The interviewer takes the chance to instil a little humour into this final less tense stage of the interview.

Susan : If I got the job Mr Ganesan, when would you expect me to start?

Interviewer : Oh, we would like the successful applicants to start as soon as possible. When could you start?

He again turns questioner and takes control of the proceedings again.

Susan : Oh, I could start on Monday if you gave me the job.

Interviewer : Well, I have got a few more applicants to interview first, so it will be a few days before we can let you know. You will get a letter from Mrs Goh, my assistant, by the end of the week, at the latest.

The interviewer now begins to tell Susan what the course of events will be after the interview.

Susan : Right. Thank you, sir.

Interviewer : It is been very nice meeting you, Susan. Thank you very much for coming all the way up from Melaka. I hope you have a nice journey home.

Mr Ganesan is now bringing the interview to a close.

Susan : Thank you, Mr Ganesan. Good-bye.

CASE STUDY TWO

Mr Jeremy Tan –
Senior Personnel
Officer of Sankyu Jasa
Department Stores.

Dinesh Maniam –
24-year-old graduate
applying for position
of Administration Executive.

ABOUT THE JOB

This interview is at a higher level. The applicant has recently graduated from a university.

COMPANY	: HAZEL
NAME OF JOB	: ADMINISTRATION EXECUTIVE
APPLICATIONS	: 300 applications received – 10 shortlisted
VACANCIES	: 1
NATURE OF JOB	: Managing an expanding firm with a big staff liaising with branch managers; decision making; to be stationed in Head Office in Singapore.
EXPECTED SALARY	: To be commensurate with qualifications and experience.
PERSON TO CONTACT	: Senior Personnel Officer

REQUIREMENTS : Degree/diploma in Marketing or Business Studies/Management in related discipline; new graduates can apply; experience not necessary but preferable; a communicator and an independent worker; willing to work very hard and for long hours; good social skills; computer and typing skills an advantage; must be very proficient in spoken and written English; having good initiative.

CLOSING DATE OF APPLICATION : April 30

DATE OF JOB COMMENCEMENT : Post to be filled as soon as possible.

> Jeremy Tan, the Senior Personnel Officer, is a very experienced interviewer. We can learn a lot from the way he handles things.

THE ADVERTISEMENT

ADMINISTRATION EXECUTIVE

We are a leading retail chain in Hong Kong, Singapore and Malaysia. We are looking for enthusiastic young candidates to grow with us in our expansion programme at our head office.

Requirements

- Degree/Diploma in Marketing or Business Administration or related discipline.
- Fresh graduates are also welcome to apply.
- Experience is not a prerequisite but would be an advantage.
- Fluency in spoken and written English is essential.
- Good communication skills and the ability to work independently.
- Have a plesant personality and the right attitude.
- Knowledge of computer and typing skills is an advantage.

Write in with a full resume, present and expected salary, contact number enclosing a recent passport-sized photo (n.r.) to:

The Senior Personnel Officer,
HAZEL'S Shopping Centres (Head Office),
Fairview Drive,
Singapore.

before 30th April.
(Only short-listed candidates will be called for an interview.)

THE COVER LETTER

29 East Street,
Pelangi Gardens,
13200 Ipoh,
Perak,
Malaysia.

March 20, 19_ _

Mr Jeremy Tan,
Senior Personnel Officer,
Hazel Shopping Centres,
Fairview Drive,
Singapore.

Dear Mr Jeremy,

Re: <u>Application for Position of Administration Executive</u>

I was excited to read your advertisement for the above post in today's edition of the New Straits Times because I believe that I possess the type of qualifications and personal qualities that you are looking for.

Hazel was often cited by the lecturers of my Business Studies course at Cardiff University as an excellent example of a go-ahead company which still managed to maintain a family atmosphere with its management staff relations. I would be delighted to have the chance to become part of such an organization. I have now successfully completed my degree course and am looking for a post which would give me the scope to develop the management and communication skills I learned as Vice-President of the Cardiff University Students' Union and as a temporary management trainee with the Lainsbury Department Store Chain in the United Kingdom. I would hope to start on a salary in the region of $4000.

I have enclosed my resume for your consideration and would like the opportunity to discuss the matter further with you. I can be contacted at 3322456.

Cordially yours,

Dinesh
(Dinesh Maniam)

RESUME

Dinesh Maniam

Full Name: Dinesh Maniam

Full Address: 29, East Street,
Pelangi Gardens,
13200 Ipoh,
Perak,
Malaysia.

Telephone: Work – 3322456
Residence – 5639800

Education:
– August 1993, BA (Hons) 2:1 Business Sudies, University of Cardiff, UK. Majored in Business Administration and Personal Management, Presented a dissertation on "Management – Staff Relations in the Large Department Stores".
– June 1992, Certificate in Computing, Cardiff University.
– July 1990, 'A' Levels: English (A), Economics (B), and History (C) at High School, Ipoh.
– June 1988, 'O' Levels: English, Malay, Maths, History, Geography and Art at High School, Ipoh.

Extra-Curricular Activities:
– Was an active member of University Athletics Club.
– Participated in debating competitions. Very active member of the University Debating Club.

Work Experience:
- Oct–Dec 1992: Lainsbury Department Store, Swansea. Gained useful practical experience in 3-month period in one of U.K.'s top department stores. This was an assessed part of the degree course. My active participation in the duties undertaken earned a Grade 'A'.
- June–Sept. 1991: Cash'n'Carry Supermarket, Cardiff. Worked on cash checkout as temporary student worker during summer vacation.

Achievements:
- 1992–1993: Elected Vice-President of Students' Union, negotiated with university authorities for improved recreational facilities.
- 1991–1992: Served as Secretary of Asian Students' Association.

Personal Details:
- Having spent 3 years in the U.K., my English is fluent.
- I consider myself to be sociable, independent and a good communicator who likes challenges.
- Available for work immediately and willing to relocate.

References:
- Academic, professional and personal references are available on request.

ACADEMIC QUALIFICATIONS

- BA (Hons) Business Studies (Cardiff, UK)
- 'A' Levels
- 'O' Levels

WORK EXPERIENCE

- Limited: work done as part of university course internship
- Temporary job

PROFESSIONAL QUALIFICATIONS

- Certificate in Computing

ACHIEVEMENTS

- Vice-President of Students' Union
- Secretary of Asian Students' Club
- University Athletics team
- School Prefect

PERSONAL DETAILS

- 3 years' in U.K., so fluent Spoken and Written English
- Sociable; good character
- Positive attitude to work
- Likes challenges

INTERESTS

- Debating
- Athletics

There is really quite a lot to look at in Mr Dinesh's application – I need to check on a number of those things and perhaps probe a little into some others.

Let us now look at the extract from the second interview and see how the graduate is interviewed.

I will be here again to help you spot the important points.

THE BEGINNING STAGE

Interviewer : Good morning, Mr Dinesh. Please come in and take a seat. I am Jeremy Tan – the Senior Personnel Officer.

A warm but formal welcome.

Dinesh : Thank you. Good morning. Pleased to meet you.

Interviewer : How did you get here? Did you drive or did you take the MRT?

A nice, easy question to break the ice.

Dinesh : I flew in from Ipoh last night and I am staying at the RELC International House. I took the MRT from Orchard Road.

Interviewer : How do you find the RELC hotel? I have heard some very good reports about it.

An opportunity to engage in informal small talk.

Dinesh : It is great. Very comfortable, quite reasonably priced. I like the place.

Interviewer : Yes, and it is so convenient since it is on Orchard Road.

Mr Tan gives Dinesh another opportunity to talk.

Dinesh : Yes, I am going to have a good look at the shops when the interview is over.

Dinesh is chatting quite freely and shows no signs of nerves.

Interviewer : Right... well, the sooner we get started the sooner you can set about your window-shopping!

Mr Tan takes the opportunity to instil a little humour into the interview and at the same time signals the end of the first stage of the interview.

Right, let us see Mr Jeremy's questioning techniques, shall we?

THE MIDDLE STAGE

Interviewer : O.K. Dinesh. I see you have been to the U.K. Where exactly did you do your 'A' levels and your first degree?

A wh-question to start the serious questioning.

Dinesh : I did my 'A' levels at a private college in K.L. Then I did my first degree in Business Studies at Cardiff. I was there for four years. I graduated with a BA (Hons) – Upper Second Class.

Interviewer : That is good. And when did you do the Computing programme?

Another wh-question as a follow-up. Note that Mr Tan is using information from his notes to ask questions.

Dinesh : Oh, that was only during my long vacation in the first year.

Interviewer : And, I see you did some temporary work while you were in the U.K. Where did you work?

Dinesh : Well, I worked with several firms. Those were short stints as part of my course. I did 3 months in the Marketing Division of a car manufacturing company; and then, I did another three months in a large supermarket as an assistant to the branch manager. That was very useful experience since I got to handle both staff and customers. It was challenging and I enjoyed it a lot.

Mr Tan focuses on a sensitive area for new graduates: work experience. But he gives Dinesh the chance to show that he does at least have some experience.

Note that Mr Tan allows his interviewee to talk. He does not think of interrupting him whilst he is developing his ideas.

Interviewer : Challenging?

Dinesh : Yes, challenging in that... you know... handling one's own staff and dealing with customers demands a different approach.

Mr Tan uses repetition to elicit more information about handling staff and customers since this will be a key feature of the job.

Interviewer : How does it differ in your opinion, Mr Dinesh?

Mr Tan begins a wh-question probe in the area of handling staff and customers.

Dinesh : Well, when you are handling staff... and then when you are handling customers... so that you see, the differences have to be taken into account.

Interviewer :	What would you do if a customer complained to you about the attitude and behaviour of a member of your staff?	*Continues the probe with a hypothetical "What if" question.*
Dinesh	: Well, first of all, I would apologise to the customer for any inconvenience and then I would...	
Interviewer :	Right, Mr Dinesh. Let me tell you more about the function of the Administration Executive at Hazel... and so you see you would be responsible for making a number of important decisions regarding staff placement and the like... So, the job is an	*Mr Tan changes the focus of the interview and adapts his role as provider of information by telling the candidate about the job.*

interesting but demanding one. What could you offer our company as a member of our staff?

Again Mr Tan comes up with a challenging job-related wh-question.

Dinesh : My work experience has taught me to take up challenges; make quick decisions; work under pressure; meet deadlines; and handle people. Besides, my knowledge of languages, I am good at English and Malay, which will help me in my job. I was a speaker at several debating competitions at my university and I think this will come in useful in communication.

It is time to listen again for Mr Tan. He allows the interviewee to develop his ideas regarding his personal qualities.

Interviewer : Mr Dinesh, what salary are you expecting?

Dinesh : As I have written in my application, I would like the company to consider my qualifications; I have got a good degree, Upper Second, from a reputed university. Besides, I have some relevant experience and computing knowledge as well. So, I would expect a good basic salary somewhere around $4000/- p.m. I am also hoping to find out about the accommodation and transport arrangements of the company.

Mr Tan seeks confirmation of the salary Mr Dinesh asked for in his cover letter, and, by doing so, elicits further views from Dinesh as to why he should get the job.

Interviewer : Well, you have the company car and a fully-furnished one-room apartment, ... I do not really have any more questions to ask at this point. Can I clarify anything further for you?

Signal that the Middle Stage is over and invitation for Dinesh to ask about the job.

THE ENDING

Dinesh : Not really, Mr Tan. I think you have covered virtually everything I need to know at this point. Thanks.

Interviewer : Well, when will you be available?

A final practical question.

Dinesh : Anytime.

Interviewer	:	That will be good. We will let you know in a fortnight's time as we have several other candidates to interview, before we make our final decisions.

Information regarding how the application will progress from here.

Dinesh	:	That is fair. I will wait for the result. I hope to be given a chance to serve your company. I am really looking forward to working with a company that is growing so rapidly.

Interviewer	:	Thank you for coming, Mr Dinesh. When are you going back to Ipoh?

Thanking and a final friendly, informal question to complete the interview.

Dinesh	:	Not for another two days. I have got

friends working
at a bank here,
so I would like
to catch up
with them.

Interviewer : Right. That will
be nice. Okay
then,
Mr Dinesh.
We will be in
contact with
you very soon.
Thank you
again for
coming.

*Leave taking and
final confirmation
of arrangements.*

Dinesh   : Thank you very
much, Mr Tan.

CASE STUDY THREE

Marvin Lee – 28-year-old graduate with 4 years' work experience applying for the post of Medical Representative.

Mr Nathan Dykes – Personnel Manager of Medi Pharma, a large pharmaceutical company.

ABOUT THE JOB

This third interview is really quite a high level affair. Marvin Lee is a graduate with good experience. He is quite a high-flier!

NAME OF POST : MEDICAL REPRESENTATIVES

APPLICATIONS : 200 received; 10 shortlisted.

VACANCIES : 2

NATURE OF JOB : Promotion and sales of pharmaceutical products; aiming at hospitals, general clinics and pharmacists throughout the country.

EXPECTED SALARY : To be commensurate with qualifications and experience.

PERKS : An attractive remuneration package of basic salary, medical insurance, incentives and other benefits will be offered to qualified candidates.

PERSON TO CONTACT : Personnel Manager

REQUIREMENTS : B.Sc in Science/Chemistry or equivalent (assistant pharmacist/diploma holder in pharmacy may be considered); 2 years' experience in a similar position.

DATE OF COMMENCEMENT : Immediately.

So, let us see how Nathan Dykes, the personnel manager, of Medi-Pharma manages to bring the best out of Marvin Lee.

THE ADVERTISEMENT

**A Well-Paid,
Exciting
And
Successful Career
Awaits You.
Call Now!**

MEDICAL REPRESENTATIVES

We are an established company involved in marketing
and distributing pharmaceutical products and are
seeking dynamic and highly motivated individuals to
fill the position of MEDICAL REPRESENTATIVES.

The successful candidate shall be responsible for the promotion and sales of pharmaceutical products to hospitals,
general practitioners and pharmacists. He should have a
university degree in science, chemistry or equivalent (assistant pharmacist/diploma holder in pharmacy may be considered). The candidates must have at least 2 years experience
in a similar position.

An attractive remuneration package of basic salary, medical
insurance, incentives and other benefits will be offered to the
qualified candidates.

Interested applicants, please forward c.v. including present
and expected salary, n.r. photograph to:

Personnel Manager,
MEDI AP PHARMA,
Lei Muk Shuest, New Territories,
Hong Kong.

Not later than Sept 25.

MEDI AP PHARMA FOR A HEALTHY LIFE

THE COVER LETTER

13 Block C,
Harvey Road,
Sea Park,
Kowloon.

September 13, 19_ _

Mr Nathan Dykes,
Personnel Manager,
Medi AP Pharma,
Lei Muk Shu Estate,
New Territories,
Hong Kong.

Dear Mr Nathan,

Your advertisement for the position of Medical Representatives which appeared in yesterday's Tribune really attracted my attention, since I seem to fulfil all of your job requirements.

I have been working for 4 years now in Hong Kong in the pharmaceutical business and the one name which I hear repeated day after day is Medi-Pharma. Such a reputation is not earned easily and I feel that the chance to work in the Medi-Pharma team would be a wonderful step forward in my career. I have been working as head of the pharmaceuticals unit of Uni-Chemicals and have also gained valuable experience in the sales and marketing functions and I feel sure that all of this hands-on expertise has given me a very sound preparation for the type of job you are advertising. My ability to work in as well as lead a team and my willingness to travel also appear to make me a suitable candidate for the position with your company. I am currently earning HK$3000 per week and would expect a salary in the region of HK$3500.

I have enclosed my curriculum vitae and photographs as requested and would be delighted to discuss my application with you. I can be contacted at 425336 (work) or 634210 (home).

Cordially yours,

Marvin
(Marvin Lee)

THE CURRICULUM VITAE

CURRICULUM VITAE: MARVIN LEE

Full Name: Marvin Lee

Full Address: 13 Block C,
Harvey Road,
Tan Park,
Kowloon.

Telephone: Work – 425336
Residence – 634210

Working Experience: – UNI CHEMICALS 1989 – Present.
Gained not only pharmaceutical experience but also developed sales and marketing expertise.
Promoted to Unit Head after $2\frac{1}{2}$ years as a team member. Responsible for all functions of the unit and reported to the Managing Director.

Achievements:
– Became the youngest Unit Head in the Company.
– Reorganised the sales/marketing function of the unit.
– Developed an efficient, cooperative team of salesmen.
Built up an extensive network of business associates in the Hong Kong area.
– Successfully administered sales/marketing and pharmaceutical functions at the same time.

Education:	– 1989 B.Sc. (Hons) Chemistry, University of Hong Kong.
	– Majored in pharmacology.
	– 1986 'A' Levels: Maths (B), Physics (B) at High School Muar, Malaysia.
Personal Information:	– Fluent in spoken and written English, Malay and Mandarin.
	– I consider myself a good mixer and communicator and a pleasant, dynamic character.
	– Since I am single, I am happy to work long hours and to relocate, if necessary.
Interests:	– Travel: Visited most countries in Asia.
	– Music: Play the piano and guitar.
References:	– Available on request.

ACADEMIC QUALIFICATIONS

- B.Sc (Hons) Chemistry
- 'A' Levels
- 'O' Levels

WORK EXPERIENCE

- 4 years in small pharmaceuticals
- Head of Unit
- Marketing Experience
- Sales Experience

PROFESSIONAL QUALIFICATIONS

- None

ACHIEVEMENTS

- Became youngest Unit Head of company.
- Reorganised Unit.
- Ran marketing/sales function as well as pharmaceutical production.

PERSONAL DETAILS

- Good English, Malay and Mandarin.
- Pleasant, dynamic personality.
- Good mixer and communicator.
- Single, happy to work long hours and to relocate, if necessary.

INTERESTS

- Travel
- Music

I have spent a lot of time looking at Marvin Lee's c.v. and cover-letter, and I have notes on what I consider to be the main points of interest. I am really quite impressed!

Let us look at the extracts from the third interview and see how the graduate is interviewed.

Let us see how Nathan Dykes handles the interview with the experienced graduate, Marvin Lee.

THE BEGINNING

Interviewer : Good morning, Mr Lee. Please take a seat. I am Nathan Dykes – the Personnel Manager of Medi AP Pharma.

Warm, friendly welcome.

Marvin Lee : Thank you, Mr Nathan. Good morning. I am pleased to meet you.

Interviewer :	Pleased to meet you too, Mr Lee. How was the journey here? Any difficulties?	*The usual ice-breaker to open with.*
Marvin Lee :	Not really. I took a cab from the Grand Mirama Hotel – it took about 25 minutes to get here through the jam, although it is only a stone's throw from here.	
Interviewer :	Yes, but still the Hong Kong traffic is not nearly as bad as in some other capital cities. I was in Kuala Lumpur the other month and the traffic jams there were really bad.	*Interviewer attempts to find common ground by talking about the candidate's own country and offers a point of comparison with Hong Kong.*
Marvin Lee :	Oh yes, that is right. Actually...	*Interviewee takes the lead and engages in small talk about traffic problems...*

Let us return to the interview now as they enter into the Middle Stage. Let us see his questioning techniques.

THE MIDDLE STAGE

Interviewer : I understand that you have been working with Uni-Chemicals for some time now. How long have you been with the company?

Marvin Lee : Precisely 4 years... and...

After the initial talk the interviewer is eager to get down to the "nitty-gritty" questions.

Interviewer : It is quite an established firm, so why are you thinking of leaving it? Why did you apply Medi AP Pharma?

He asks a direct wh-question to find out the applicant's reasons for wanting to join his company.

Marvin Lee : I guess I needed a change. Somehow I like to travel around and do not like being stationed in one place too long. I like to move around in my job, and this job in your company would give me a chance to travel to other branches out of this town; whereas in my present company I do not get a chance to travel out of this town at all.

Interviewer : (pause)

Marvin Lee : Also, Mr Nathan, if you will allow me to add, honestly, I think your company is expanding faster and this would certainly give me more scope to develop myself too...

Silent pause to elicit more information on this subject.

Interviewer : What is the nature of your present job? What do you do exactly?

Interviewer wants to find out more about the candidate's working experience.

Marvin Lee : I actually handle everything to do with pharmaceutical products; I meet prospective clients; ...

Intervewer : Really. Where do you find them?

Interviewer probes with another wh-question.

Marvin Lee : I try to call on clinics to market our products. I have ample contacts in this town. But you see, it is limited to just this area. It is a small firm really. Also, I think I have enough experience to deal with hospitals and other big pharmaceutical firms.

Interviewer : What are your other duties in Uni-chemicals?

The probe continues.

Marvin Lee : Well, I ...

Interviewer : You are used to working in a small firm; so, how would you fit into a larger organization like ours?

The interviewer changes the tone and asks a really demanding question regarding the candidate's suitability for the job.

Marvin Lee : ...Fitting into a big company should not be much of a problem. Does not almost everyone begin that way? Is that not a natural progression? It is like having an addition to the family too. Besides, I feel my four-years' experience at my present job and my contacts will assist me in this new job. I love meeting people. I am proficient in English, Malay and Mandarin,

Having asked a difficult question, the interviewer now allows the candidate to develop his answer uninterrupted.

and should find
this an asset.
And as I said
earlier I love
challenges,
and I think
working in a
bigger
company like
this one would
suit my kind of
personality.

Interviewer : That is good.
What do you
know about
Medi AP
Pharma? How
did you find out
about us?

*Quite pleased with the
candidate's response he
follows up with a less
demanding but nevertheless
probing question.*

Marvin Lee : I talked to
several staff
working here;
and I am aware
of the kind of
jobs they are
doing here.
Most of my
friends speak
favourably of
your company;
and I guess
they have
influenced me
here. They feel

that I should work here as I particularly like to deal with the promotion of products...

Interviewer : Let me tell you a little more about the job here Mr Lee... You know, we work a six-day week, while yours is a five-day week only. Would this be a problem to you as you are already used to a holiday every Saturday?

Interviewer changes role and begins to inform the applicant about the nature of the job. Interviewer finishes his job description off with a question regarding the candidate's willingness to fit in.

Marvin Lee : I am aware of this because my friends working here have told me this. So, it is not news to me. If I like the job, I am willing to work hard. I like to grow with a reputed company, and if I have to work on a Saturday, I guess, I would soon be used to this idea and would acclimatize myself to this.

Interviewer : I see from the application forms the expected salary. Would you work for anything less than that?

Interviewer follows up with another 'testing' question.

Marvin Lee : Of course, it would be ridiculous moving to a job that offers you a lower salary. I would certainly be laughed at by my family members and my colleagues, especially since I have a job with a good salary. But, right now,

maybe I should
look at the
other benefits
and incentives
you have
mentioned
in your
advertisement.
As your
company is
growing fast, I
would look
ahead! I am
certainly more
interested in
the long term
working
conditions. I
also like the
idea of
travelling
around to other
branches both
within and
outside the
country...

Yet again, the interviewer listens carefully and politely to the interviewee's long response to a "thorny" question.

THE ENDING

Interviewer : Is there anything you would like to know about the company?

Interviewer gives the candidate the opportunity to ask further questions.

Marvin Lee : What is the staff enrolment of this branch?

Interviewer : Well, as you know we have 8 branches in this country and 3 overseas. Our staff enrolment for this branch is 80. In all, we have around 900 employees all together...

Interviewer gives a full answer to the question.

Marvin Lee : Really, that is quite a large organization.

Interviewer : Anything else I can tell you, Mr Lee?

A further invitation to ask questions.

Marvin Lee : No, I think I have got a very clear picture of things. Thank you, Mr Nathan.

Interviewer : Okay then. Just one more thing. I would like to ask you when you would be available, as I understand you are still working.

Interviewer elicits information regarding availability.

Marvin Lee : Well, I would have to be fair to my present company and give them the usual one-month notice. But, frankly, I would hesitate to do that.

Interviewer : Yes, I understand that Mr Lee. We will get in touch with you during the next couple of days. You have given us your contact number. You will be hearing from us soon.

Gives information as to when interviewee will be informed about the results of the interview.

Thank you for coming. It has been very nice talking to you.

Warm, friendly end to interview.

Marvin Lee : Thank you for inviting me to the interview. I will be looking forward to hearing from you. Bye.